Usborne
Build your own
GIANT BUGS
Sticker Book

Illustrated by Gong Studios

Designed by Claire Thomas and Marc Maynard

Written by Sam Smith

Consultants: Dr. Margaret Rostron and Dr. John Rostron

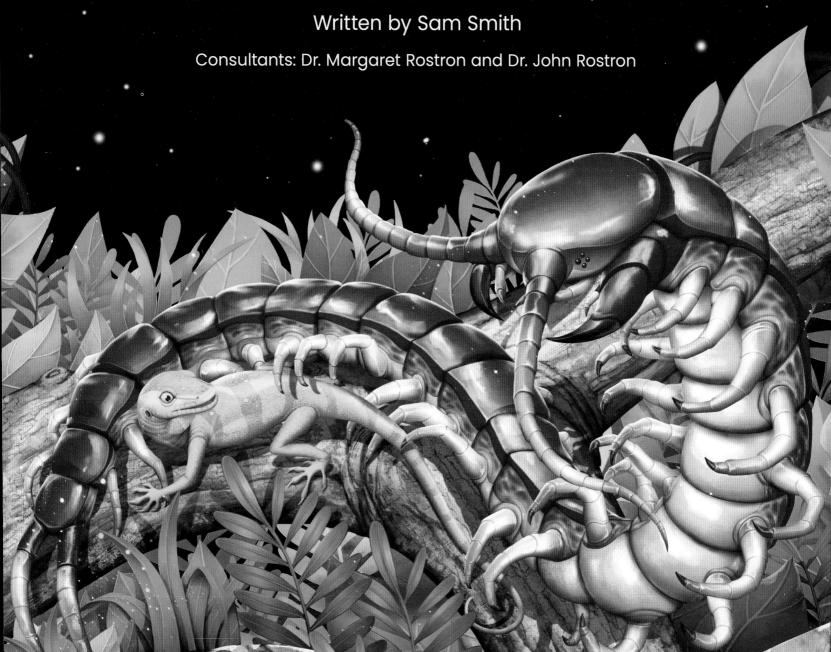

GOLIATH BEETLE

This beetle can lift over 800 times its own weight – that's like a human lifting ten elephants! Using its horns like a shovel, it's tossed aside its rivals to feast on this sweet tree sap.

STATISTICS

• SCIENTIFIC NAME:	*Goliathus goliatus*
• SIZE:	11cm (4.3in) long
• HABITAT:	African tropical forests and savannas
• DIET:	Tree sap, fruit

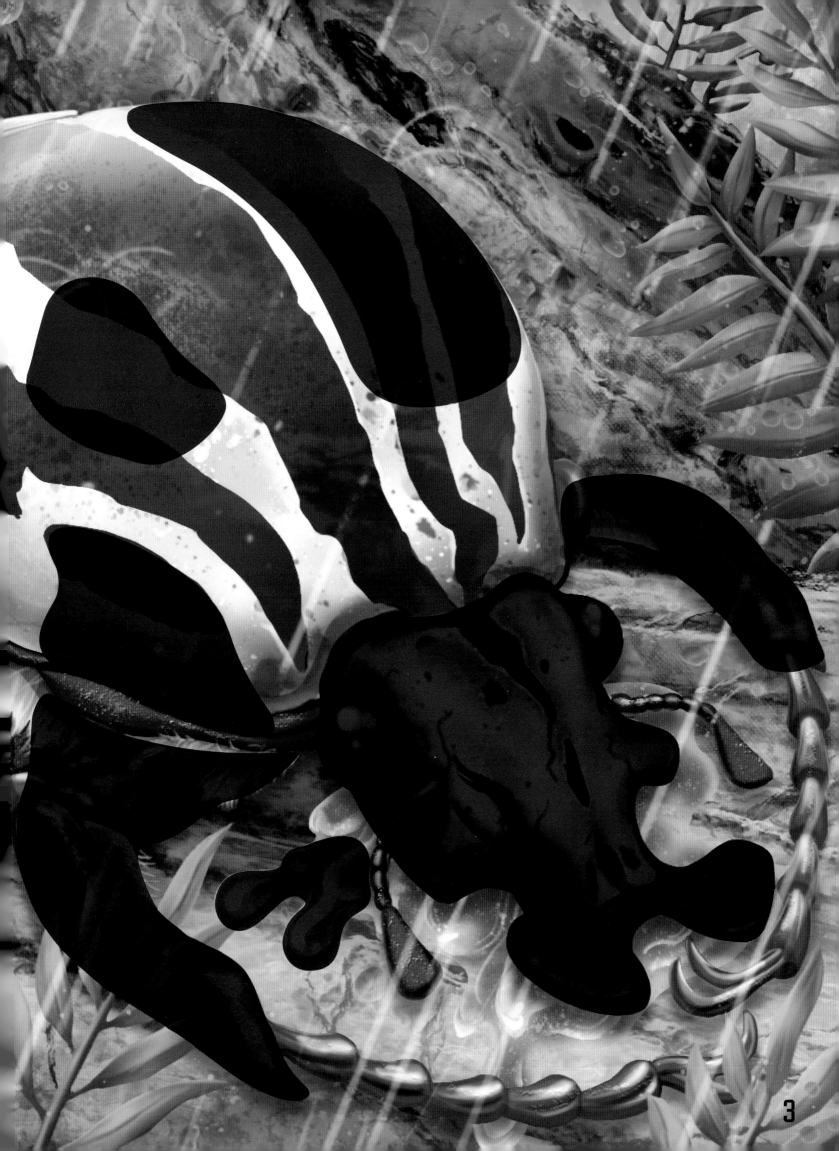

HICKORY HORNED DEVIL

The birds leave this giant, spiky caterpillar well alone. Hungrily gobbling up leaves, it grows huge as it strips whole branches bare – then it crawls down and burrows into the ground. Nine months later, a beautiful moth will emerge.

STATISTICS

• SCIENTIFIC NAME:	*Citheronia regalis*
• SIZE:	15cm (5.9in) long
• HABITAT:	Deciduous forests in USA
• DIET:	Hickory, walnut and persimmon leaves

RAINBOW MILKWEED LOCUST

Darkening the sky like a monsoon cloud, these swarming insects devour poisonous plants in their millions. This food makes each locust highly toxic, and its bright body is a warning to enemies: "If you eat me, it's the last thing you'll ever do..."

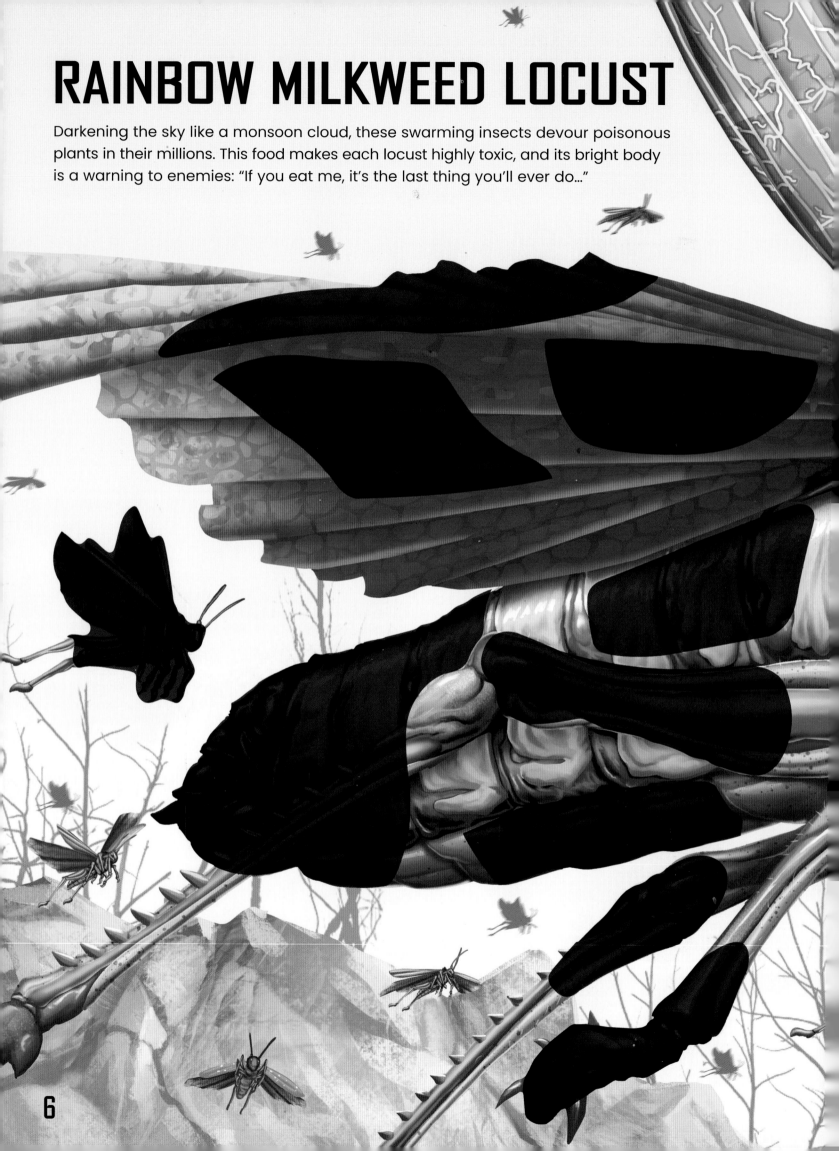

STATISTICS

• SCIENTIFIC NAME:	*Phymateus saxosus*
• SIZE:	7cm (2.8in) long; 12cm (4.7in) wingspan
• HABITAT:	Lightly forested areas in Africa
• DIET:	Milkweed leaves and other toxic plants

GOLIATH BIRDEATER

Meet the most gigantic spider on the planet. It pounces with fangs as long as a lion's claws and drags the prey back to its burrow. There, it spins a huge web to lay its eggs – 200 of them that will soon hatch more of these hairy giants!

STATISTICS

• SCIENTIFIC NAME:	*Theraphosa blondi*
• SIZE:	13cm (5.1in) long; 28cm (11in) legspan
• HABITAT:	South American rainforests
• DIET:	Insects, mice, lizards, frogs, snakes

JUNGLE NYMPH

CHIRP, CHIRP, CHIRP... When danger is near, this insect opens wide its scissor-like legs, and rustles its wings noisily. If that warning sound is ignored, the legs snap shut at the slightest touch, skewering the attacker on their deadly spikes.

STATISTICS

- **SCIENTIFIC NAME:** *Heteropteryx dilatata*
- **SIZE:** 17cm (6.7in) long
- **HABITAT:** Rainforests of South-East Asia
- **DIET:** Leaves of tropical trees

AMAZONIAN GIANT CENTIPEDE

When darkness falls, there's nowhere to hide from this many-legged nightmare. Scuttling through the undergrowth, it finds a tasty lizard. Then the venomous, needle-sharp pincers shut tight, and the prey stops struggling.

STATISTICS

- **SCIENTIFIC NAME:** *Scolopendra gigantea*
- **SIZE:** 30cm (11.8in) long
- **HABITAT:** Rainforests of South America
- **DIET:** Insects, lizards, birds, bats, tarantulas

DEVIL'S FLOWER MANTIS

Here's a stealthy ninja of the insect world. Disguised as a flower, it stays perfectly still and watches with five unblinking eyes. As soon as a fly buzzes by, its legs strike out to snatch it from the sky.

STATISTICS

- **SCIENTIFIC NAME:** *Idolomantis diabolica*

- **SIZE:** 13cm (5.1in) long

- **HABITAT:** Wooded grasslands of East Africa

- **DIET:** Flies

EXECUTIONER WASP

This lone female's gnashing jaws chew up wood to sculpt her nest, and turn prey to mush with their saliva. Hunting to feed her hungry brood, she'll soon be the queen of a whole colony.

STATISTICS

• SCIENTIFIC NAME:	*Polistes carnifex*
• SIZE:	3.3cm (1.3in) long
• HABITAT:	Tropical forests without heavy rain
• DIET:	Caterpillars, nectar

GIANT MESQUITE BUG

Instead of trying to hide, these young bugs cluster together so that they look like one big monster. If an enemy still dares to come too close, they fire out a spray that's toxic enough to kill a tarantula.

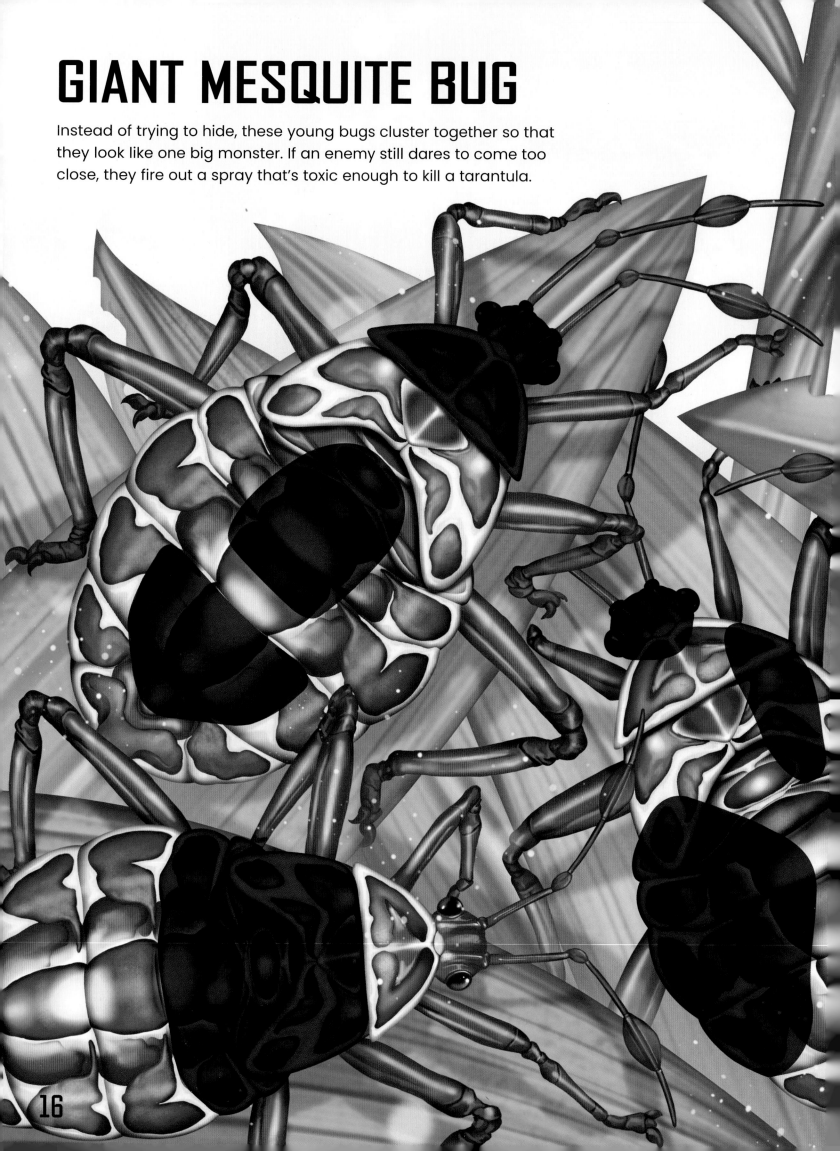

STATISTICS

- **SCIENTIFIC NAME:** *Thasus neocalifornicus*
- **SIZE:** 3cm (1.2in) long
- **HABITAT:** Central and North American deserts
- **DIET:** Seedpods and sap of mesquite trees

GIANT WĒTĀ

This hamster-sized cricket is one of the heaviest insects on Earth. Unable to jump or fly, it shuffles slowly through the trees, listening for danger with ears located on its knees.

STATISTICS

• SCIENTIFIC NAME:	*Deinacrida heteracantha*
• SIZE:	11cm (4.3in) long; 17.5cm (6.9in) legspan
• HABITAT:	Forests on one island in New Zealand
• DIET:	Forest leaves

ROSEATE SKIMMER

Perched on a reed, this agile dragonfly scans the skies in all directions. Once its giant eyes lock onto a target, there's no escape – it dances after it like a deadly ballerina, predicting each move with lethal precision.

STATISTICS

• **SCIENTIFIC NAME:**	*Orthemis ferruginea*
• **SIZE:**	5.5cm (2.2in) long
• **HABITAT:**	Open water in N. and S. America
• **DIET:**	Insects its own size or smaller

TARANTULA HAWK WASP

This ferocious blue wasp fights tarantulas (see bottom left), and it never loses. Paralyzing its prey with a well-placed sting, it lays a single egg on top, then buries it. When the hungry larva hatches, it will slowly eat the entire spider.

STATISTICS

• SCIENTIFIC NAME:	*Pepsis grossa*
• SIZE:	5.1cm (2in) long
• HABITAT:	Desert scrub in N. and S. America
• DIET:	Nectar, tarantulas

ATLAS MOTH

As this insect rests among jungle leaves, a hungry lizard creeps closer...
BAM! Suddenly the moth twitches its wingtips so that they look like
the heads of angry snakes, and the frightened predator flees.

STATISTICS

• SCIENTIFIC NAME:	*Attacus atlas*
• SIZE:	24cm (9.4in) wingspan
• HABITAT:	Dry tropical forests of South-East Asia
• DIET:	Adults don't eat; caterpillars eat leaves

GLOSSARY

- **BROOD:** a family of young insects that all hatch from the same group of eggs
- **COLONY:** a society of insects where each one has its own role and status
- **DECIDUOUS:** a tree that's deciduous loses its leaves each year
- **LARVA:** a young insect that hasn't yet changed into its adult form, for example a caterpillar
- **MONSOON:** a season of heavy rainstorms

- **NINJA:** a secret agent in ancient Japan who was highly skilled in stealth and martial arts
- **PREDATOR:** an animal that hunts
- **PREY:** an animal that's hunted
- **SAVANNA:** tropical grassland with scattered trees
- **SWARMING:** flying in a large, dense group
- **TOXIC:** poisonous
- **VENOMOUS:** describes an animal that produces poison which it injects by biting or stinging

Edited by Sam Taplin

Digital manipulation by Keith Furnival